DESMOND DURST AT HIS DIRTY

Written by William Wiesner

Illustrated by Mikaila Maidment

For MOM and POW
for planting a seed,
and to Mr. Little for
cultivating a dream.
-W.W.

For Ollie, my muse,
always.
-M.M.

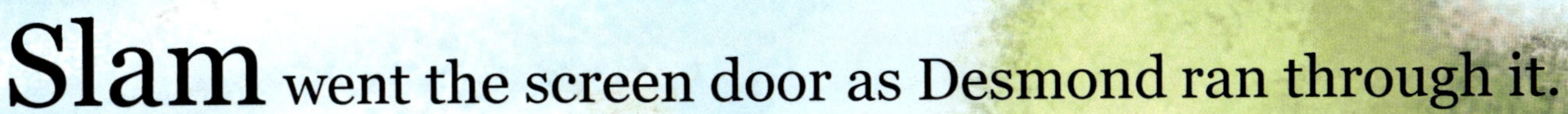

Slam went the screen door as Desmond ran through it.

Desmond Durst loved being dirty; the filthier the better! The only thing he loved more than being dirty was his dirt pile - the perfect place to dig, build, and demolish. It was finally summer and Desmond planned to spend every minute of it romping in the dirt.

"I'll be right out!" yelled Mom through the kitchen window.

You see, not far from Desmond's favorite spot was Mom's favorite place to play - her garden. It was a beautiful garden filled with loads of vegetables.

Desmond was hard at work getting as dirty as he could when Mom entered the backyard headed straight for her garden.

It wasn't long before Desmond heard her scream.

“Ahhh! Those pesky rabbits have been in my garden again!”she wailed.

Desmond couldn’t help but smile; the battle Mom waged against the rabbits made him chuckle.

As Mom stomped to the shed determined to find something to deter the rabbits and something else to revive her nibbled plants, she walked past Desmond. He was now in the process of making a dirt angel.

"Goodness, Desmond! I see you're going to need a bath tonight!" Mom said. "You have enough dirt on your head to sprout spinach," she mumbled as she returned to the house.

Love Your Garden
SIMPLY IN SEASON
Forgotten Fruits
GARDEN Shortcuts
Gardening Techniques
SUSTAINABLE LANDSCAPING
GARDEN MAGIC

Desmond entered the house that evening exhausted from a gritty day in the dirt; he snuck past his mother who was busy researching ways to keep those robbing rabbits out of her garden.

Slam went the screen door as Desmond ran through it.

"Not so fast young man," said Mom as she followed him into the backyard.

"You went to bed without taking a bath last night; if you're not careful you will sprout potatoes from your ears," Mom said.

Desmond didn't even slow down as he continued to the mound.

"You're taking one tonight!" Mom demanded.

Desmond dove into the dirt.

Mom threw up her hands in defeat and walked over to her garden to inspect her prized plants. Another loud scream rang through the neighborhood; the rabbits had been back.

Desmond spent the entire day in the dirt; by now there wasn't an inch of him that wasn't saturated with soil. Tonight he would have to be sure Mom was good and busy if he was going to make it past her without a bath. *Home free* he thought as he crawled into bed. Another dirty day down.

Slam went the screen door as Desmond ran through it.

"Stop right there Desmond Durst," hollered Mom. "You went to bed last night without taking a bath. Just look at you; you're filthy!"

Desmond smirked as he continued to the mound.

"You're taking a bath tonight," Mom said sternly. "You're covered in so much dirt you could grow your own garden."

Desmond couldn't help but feel pleased with himself; after all, it was his goal to have the dirtiest summer ever! Today would be an even dirtier day than ever before; it was time for mud.

“Mom, where’s the hose?” Desmond bellowed across the yard.

“It’s around the house behind my garden,” Mom replied. “I’ll get it for you,” she hollered back.

This time the shriek Mom let out stopped Desmond in his tracks.

“They’ve destroyed it; nothing’s left of my beautiful garden,” Mom sobbed.

It was true; the rabbits had crunched, chomped, and chewed every single plant.

“Want me to dig holes for new seeds?” Desmond asked.

Mom shook her head and said, “It’s too late to plant now. It’s summer. The rabbits have won.”

She turned and moped to the house. Desmond shrugged, grabbing the hose; he had mud to make.

The fireflies zoomed through the yard around Desmond; the day had come to an end. It would take stealth to get past Mom and up to bed undetected. Desmond slinked into the house and surveyed the scene. Mom's gardening books were scattered in their usual spot, but Mom was nowhere to be seen - the coast was clear.

"Gotcha!" Mom laughed as she yanked Desmond into the bathroom."Desmond Durst, you are the worst! I thought you might forget to take a bath again tonight so I filled the tub for you. Use soap and don't forget to scrub behind your ears," Mom said.

Desmond stared into the clear water, a reflection he didn't recognize staring back at him.

He giggled as he undressed. Now he couldn't wait to see how dirty he could make the tub. He put one foot in and watched the water change from clear to murky brown with just a wiggle of his toes.

He got the rest of the way in and the urge to play in the dirty water took over.

Time passed and the warm water soon turned cold. Desmond glanced at the untouched bar of soap on the edge of the tub; his smirk returned as he stood to grab a towel.

He quickly dried, shoved his dirt-covered towel in the hamper, and ran snickering to his room.

After a good night's sleep, he would be ready to renew his dirt layer with another day on the mound.

Desmond awoke the next morning to a tickle in his ear. He put his hand to his ear and felt something strange. He quickly plucked it, and there in his hand was a little green vine. Desmond shrugged and threw the vine aside; he had better things to do than worry about little vines; his dirt mound was waiting.

Slam went the screen door as Desmond ran through it.

"I'll be right out!" Mom yelled after him.

Desmond was pleased to see the water-soaked mound from the day before had dried out overnight.

Mom walked up carrying a big glass of water.

“I want you to drink plenty of water today,
and be sure to soak up some bright summer sun -
but not too much; I wouldn’t want you to wilt...
I mean, get overheated,” Mom said.

She handed Desmond the glass of water and pranced back into the house.

Just then Desmond noticed another vine poking out of the sleeve of his t-shirt.

He went to pluck it like he had the first, but when he reached his hand up his sleeve, he found this little vine held tight.

Desmond lifted his t-shirt to get to the root of the problem.

As Desmond began to pull up his shirt, he beheld an alarming sight - the little vine was not alone!

Shoots had grown around his chest, from his belly button sprang tiny buds, and worst of all there were sprouts peaking from the waist of his shorts. Desmond jerked his shirt back down in a panic; could it be true? Had he collected enough dirt to grow his own garden? Desmond, not wanting Mom to be right, slowly brought his hand to his ear...

“Oh, No! Potatoes!” Desmond yipped as he felt behind his ears. He would have to hide his discovery from Mom; no way was he going to let Mom be right.

He ran to the shed to hide. By the time he reached the shed, the vines were growing so fast there was no way he could hide them.

Desmond could feel the seams of his clothing beginning to stretch from the growing vines. The vines wriggled through the stitching and surged from his sleeves and up from his collar.

Desmond didn’t have a chance; the vines couldn’t be corralled.

Just when Desmond thought things couldn't get worse he felt a tingle take over his body; it started at his toes and worked its way up to the tip of his nose. Then, like someone had turned on a light switch, the vines exploded with vegetables. There were carrots and cabbages, radishes and rutabagas, peppers and potatoes.

The door of the shed flew open as Desmond ran for the house; it was time to get Mom!

When the screen door slowly opened, Mom watched with wide eyes as her son entered- a giant tangle of vines and veggies. As soon as Desmond's eyes met his mother's, he knew she would come to his rescue.

"All this can be fixed with a little soap and a long soak in the tub," she said.

The de-veggication process took hours, but soon Desmond was thoroughly picked, plucked, and pruned.

As Desmond entered the tub he could feel the clean water go to work; he let out a sigh of relief as he watched his body return to normal. Desmond grabbed the bar of soap and began scrubbing - he wasn't getting out until he was squeaky clean.

Desmond stood in the bathroom toweling off when Mom hollered up from the kitchen.

"Dinner's almost ready... and you've been remembering to brush your teeth, haven't you?"

Made in the USA
Monee, IL
17 February 2022